T0317779

BEST OF
POOL DESIGN

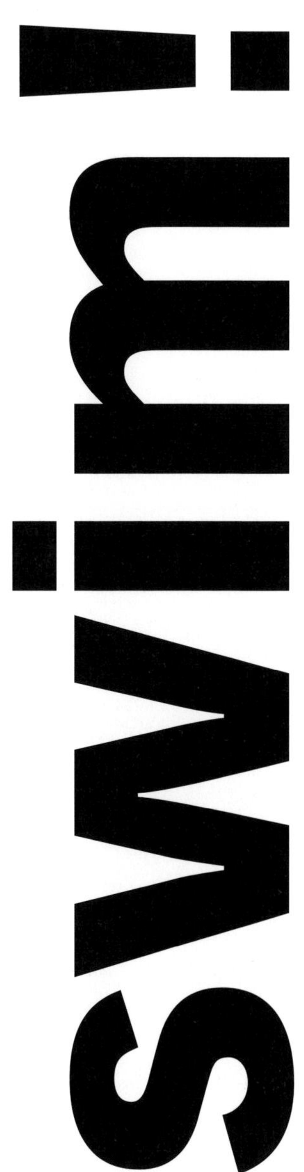

Imprint
The Deutsche Nationalbibliothek lists this publication in the Deutsche Nationalbibliografie; detailed bibliographical data are available on the internet at http://dnb.d-nb.de.

ISBN 978-3-03768-063-6

www.braun-publishing.ch

1st edition 2011

Project coordinator: Judith Vonberg
Editorial staff: Jennifer Kozak, Manuela Roth
Text editing english: Judith Vonberg
Introduction: Dagmar Glück
Translation: Geoffrey Steinherz
Graphic concept: Michaela Prinz

BEST OF
POOL DESIGN

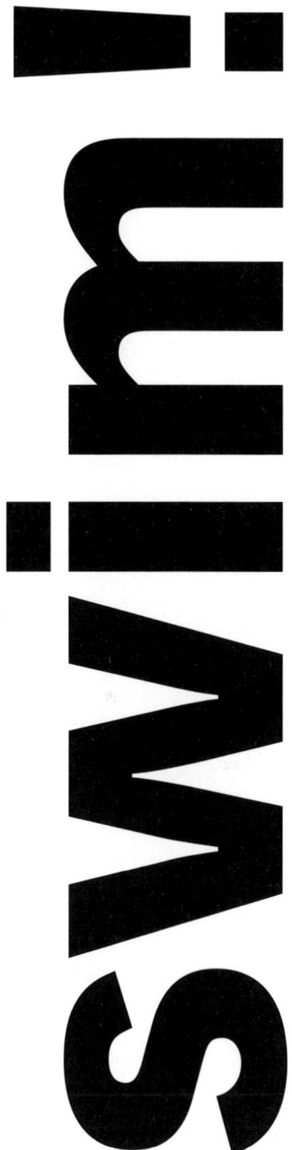

BRAUN

Preface

Dagmar Glück

The swimming pool as status symbol of the rich and famous that only serves as a backdrop for glamorous parties and romance waiting to be filmed is a cliché of yesterday. Today the swimming pool stands for wellness and is more than ever in demand. Thanks to technological progress and new materials, owning one has become affordable for broader layers of the population, while the public swimming pool is also undergoing a renaissance and could set trends.

The creativity of architects who know how to stage the element of water has changed the image of the swimming pool. *Swim! Best of Pool Design* presents 51 current projects from around the world. Immersed in the innovative designs of prominent architects and up and coming designers from Singapore to Milan and Berlin, to Buenos Aires, viewers are able to experience the most varied approaches to the exciting subject of water.

Swimming stimulates the circulation and spares the joints. As a sport it fits in perfectly with the recent wellness trend, because it offers movement as well as relaxation. Every swimmer has his own style and pace. Top athletes hone their movement sequences in order to set records, hobby swimmers swim their leisurely laps and some vacationers just want to drift. The needs of the swimmers are in the foreground of the planning of a pool. The spectrum of design ranges from the Olympic level swimming facility to the pool as entrée for the hotel business to the public pool which increases its attraction as a function of individual design.

Precious and natural materials are employed. Colored exposed concrete, wood, mosaic tiles or natural stone have made the sparkling turquoise bauble a thing of the past. The new criteria are organic forms and the harmonic inclusion of the pool in the overall design. The reflection allows for the interaction the building and the water. The pool incorporates the facade and in the truest sense of the word creates a flowing transition to the garden. The coming trend is the nature pool, replete with the rain water conditioning systems and solar units called for by the increased environmental demand for energy efficient solutions.

By contrast in the luxury segment a kind of wasteful decadence has set in: The Infinity Pool. At least one edge of the pool lies a few millimeters below the water level. This gives the surface an endless effect that merges with the horizon. In addition to an expensive circulation system this effect requires a spectacular and at the same time difficult location from a structural engineering standpoint, like a cliff or the roof of a high-rise. This expensive species of pool is inspired by the terrace shaped rice field of Bali and is frequently to be found in exclusive luxury resorts.

Public pools were for a long time less comfortable and aesthetically appealing than hotel pools. The neglected sports pool which was prevalent until the 1980's featured a lot of chlorine and direct light to suggest hygiene. Leisure and adventure pools boomed in the 1990's. Lots of glass, sun filled spaces and south sea props evoked the holiday feeling. But the number of visitors to such facilities is declining because they do not fulfill the desire for wellness.

A retrospective look shows that wellness has a long tradition. The ancient Romans considered water a valuable commodity. They executed an architectural master work in order to take advantage of it. They brought the water into the city via aqueducts, where it was warmed in the thermae. These public bathing facilities were a significant aspect of social life of the city. In addition they offered a broad spectrum of massage, gymnastics and beauty treatments.

Today's pool design returns to these origins. In their pool design Matteo Thun & Partners draw on and reinterpret the thousand year old spa and thermae tradition of Meran. Specially treated wood and local stone are the prevailing building materials. The surfaces look as if water has left its mark over the centuries. The Meran thermae is consciously oriented to the local and pristine. The Atelier Jean Nouvel "Aquatic Center Les Bains des Docks" also displays the mediterranean touch. The pools are clad with small white marble tiles which glisten in the sunlight. Although the pool is almost entirely done in white, the design features enormous visual variety. The viewer's gaze is diverted to the interior of the pool by niches, projections, sinks and changes in direction. Singular architecture becomes the secret to success of the modern pools. Another example is the "Bernaqua" adventure pool. With its slants and angles, metal, wood and glass and dynamic bathing landscape unfolding in unconventional angles it bears the unmistakable signature of Daniel Libeskind. The sharp edged, high main hall sets an almost sacral tone that pays homage to the water as the source of life.

All the designs presented in *Swim!* are an invitation to leap into the wetness. They provide an impressive demonstration of how, in addition to the tactile, a pool design can stimulate the visual sense. Water and architecture enter into an aesthetic symbiosis, which unites their contrasting qualities. Where architecture is opaque and static, water is transparent and dynamic. When water becomes an object of architecture, the result is the special excitement which characterizes the charm of the pool design.

A **path** of stepping **stones** links the **lounge** and kitchen **space** across the **pool**.

A **unique style** of life in a white **world** of **mirrors** and **glass**.

Place is the key notion here, with all its emotional and spatial connotations.

Designed with **respect** for and in **harmony** with the **natural** environment.

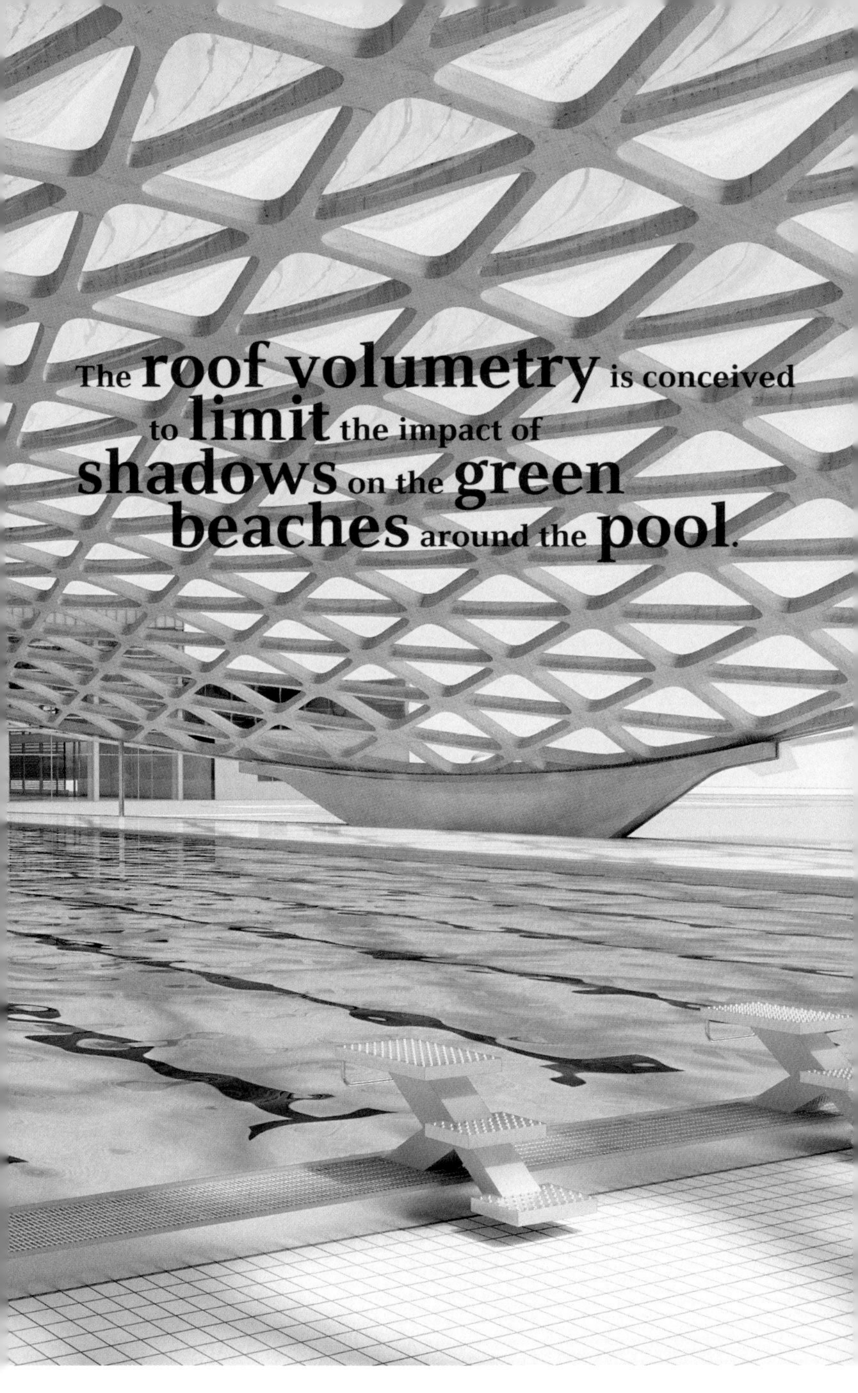

The **roof volumetry** is conceived to **limit** the impact of **shadows** on the **green beaches** around the **pool**.

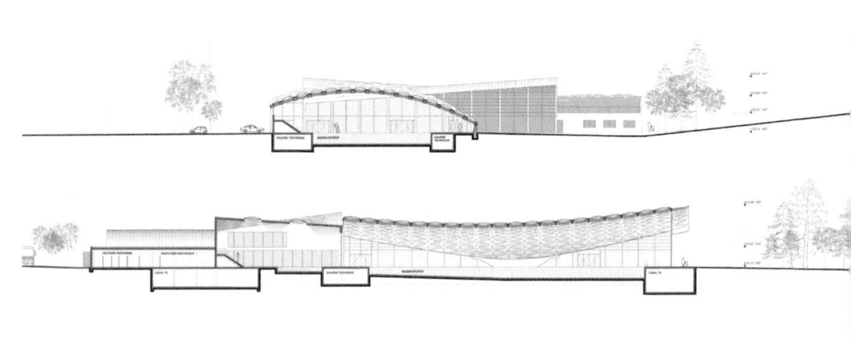

Following the Roman model, a variety of bathing experiences are offered.

3
2
1

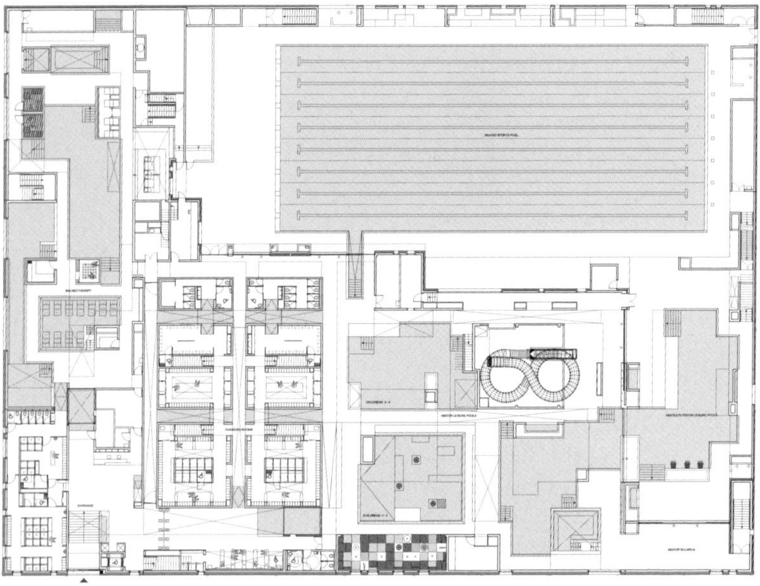

HEATED SPORTS POOL
BALNEOTHERAPY
CHANGING ROOMS
INDOOR LEISURE POOLS
HEATED OUTDOOR LEISURE POOLS
ENTRANCE
INDOOR SOLARIUM

pataugeoire

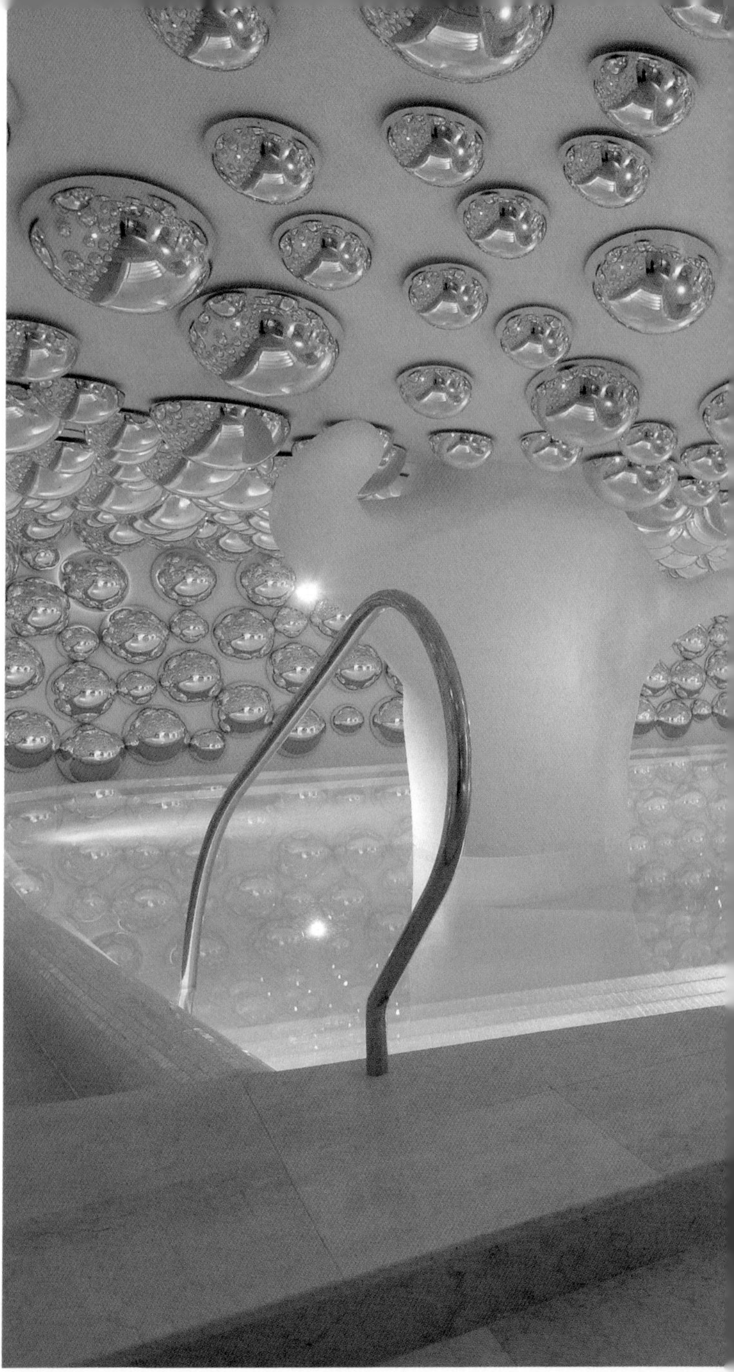

The **visitor** is placed in a **counter-reality** which enables him to **rediscover** himself and to **establish** a new mind and body **balance**.

Water merges with and overflows
black granite,
a wooden platform
penetrating the boundary and
encroaching on the water.

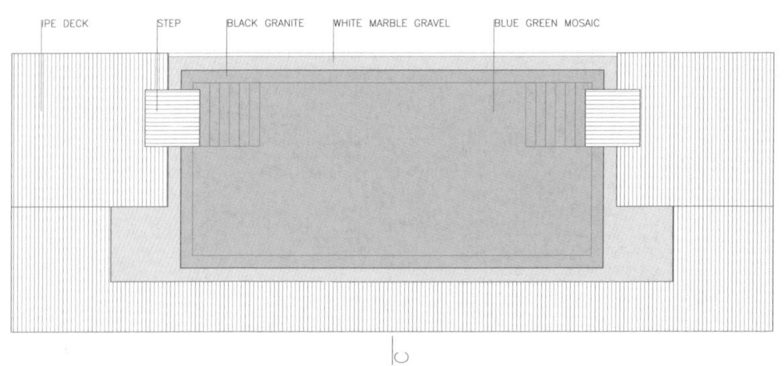
IPE DECK
STEP
BLACK GRANITE
WHITE MARBLE GRAVEL
BLUE GREEN MOSAIC

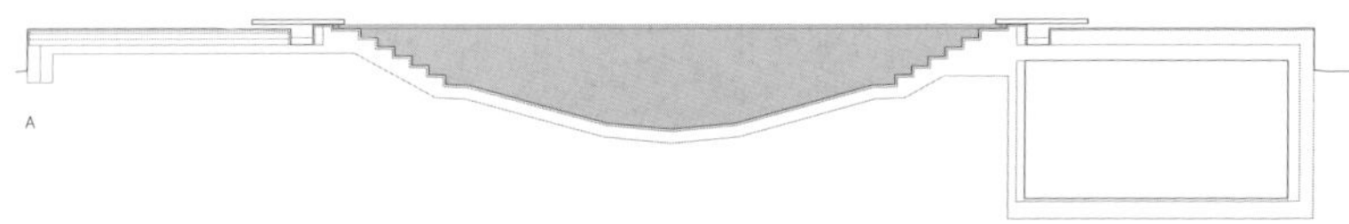
A

Lending a new **focus** to the **Spree**, the **ship** gives the impression of **swimming** in the **river** itself.

When **swimming** in the **outside** pool, **water** and **horizon** seem to **merge** into one.

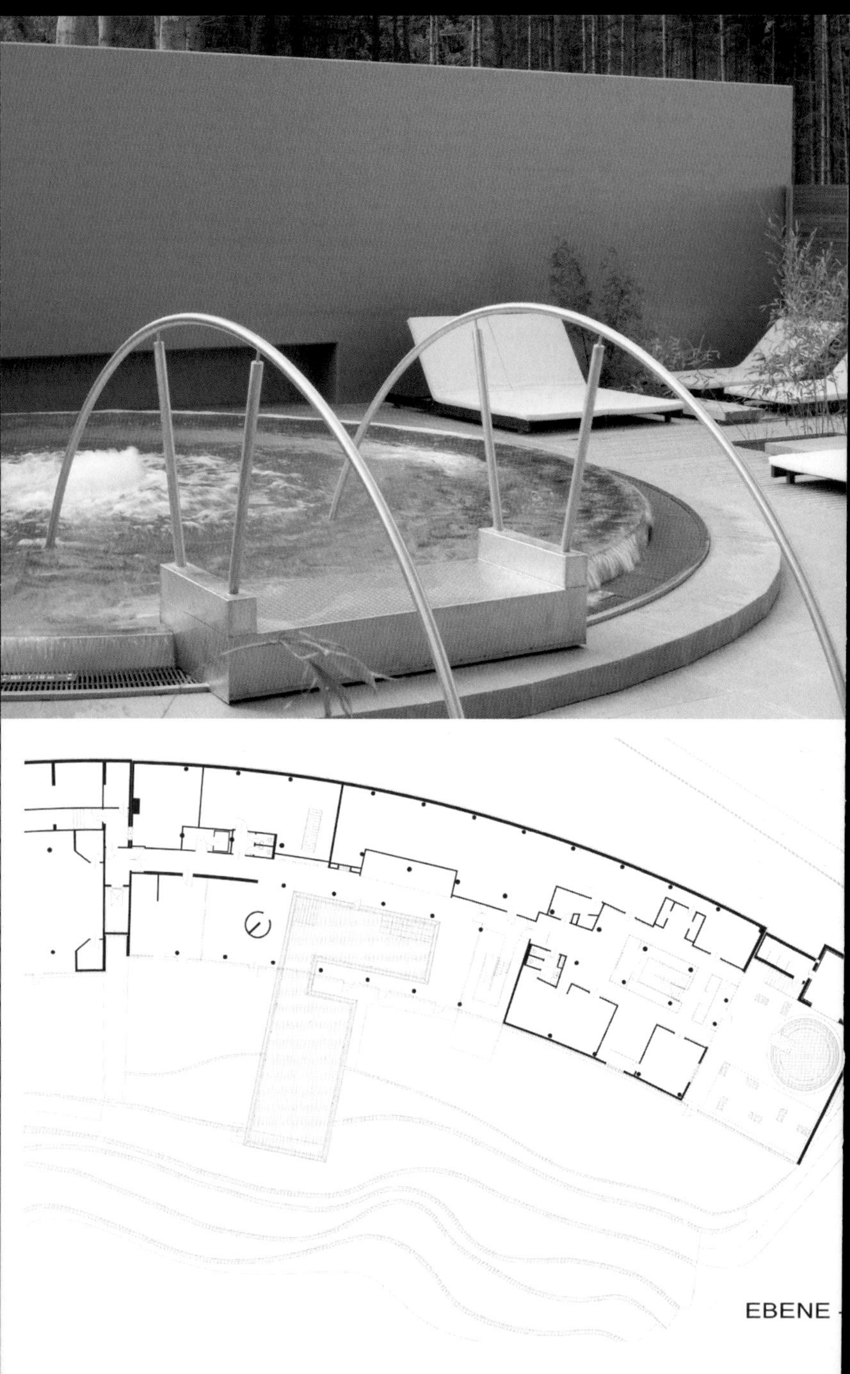

EBENE

Two petroleum water tanks act as pools, offering superb views of the Caribbean.

MEX
HOTEL BÁSICO
LAT NTE 20° 37.5' 10"
LAT PTE 87° 03.03' 8"

MEX
HOTEL BASICO
LAT NTE 20° 37.5' 10'
LAT PTE 87° 03.03' 8'

The **element** of **water** is experienced in a **multitude** of new ways.

fitness
sauna
spa

The house **opens** in the **middle**, allowing **water** and **light** to **enter**.

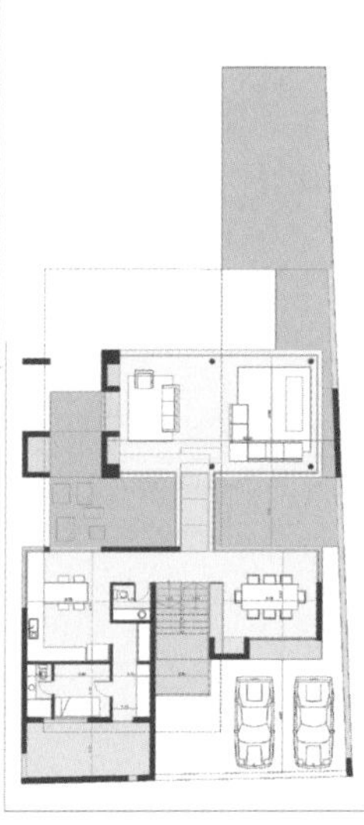

The swimming **pool** is **open** and **luminous.**

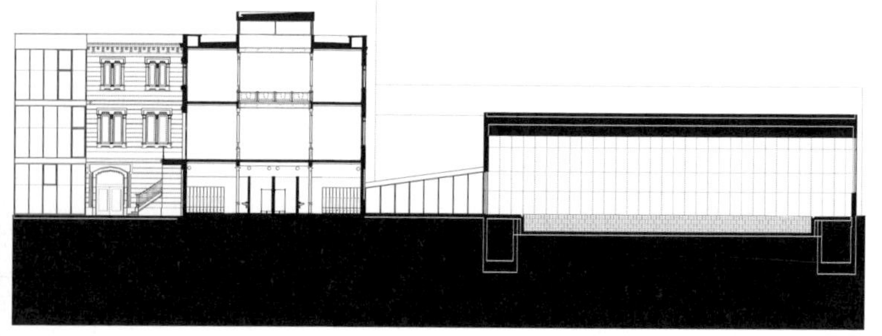

The 45 meter infinity edged pool merges seamlessly with the ocean beyond.

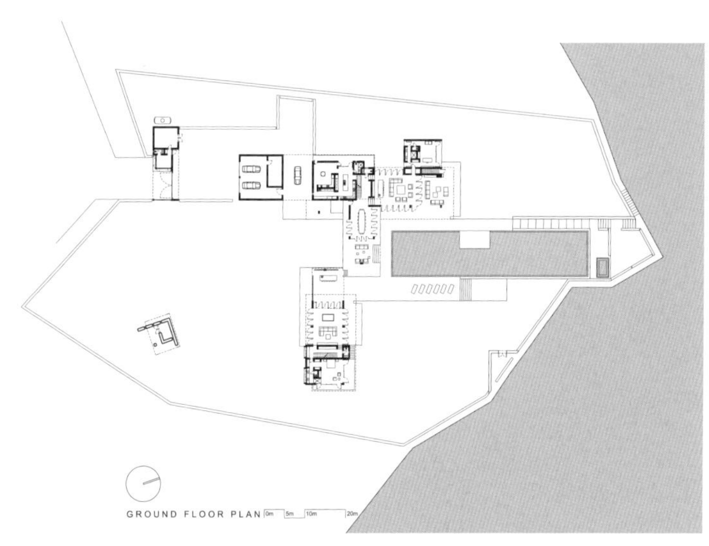
GROUND FLOOR PLAN
0m
5m
10m
20m

As a terraced landscape the Harbor Bath completes the transition from land to water.

The Copenhagen
Little Mermaid
sculpture offers an experience
of Danish life in China.

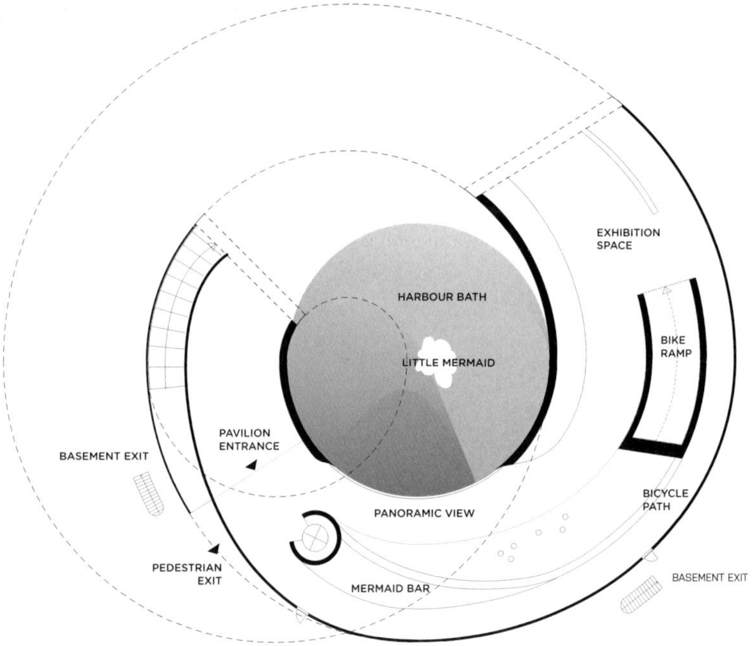

EXHIBITION SPACE

HARBOUR BATH

BIKE RAMP

LITTLE MERMAID

PAVILION ENTRANCE

BASEMENT EXIT

BICYCLE PATH

PANORAMIC VIEW

PEDESTRIAN EXIT

MERMAID BAR

BASEMENT EXIT

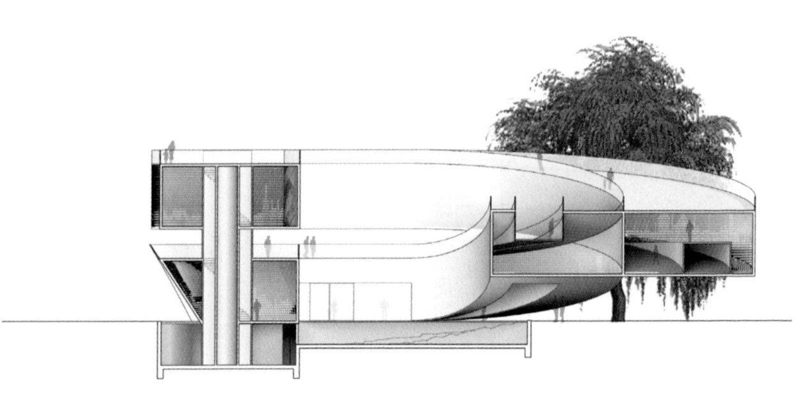

Billowy **white canopies** offer relief from the **sun** during the day; at **night**, the pool doubles as a **club lounge**.

FROM YOU

WAY FROM YOU

The **pool** is **integrated** on an **upper** level in the **protected** garden.

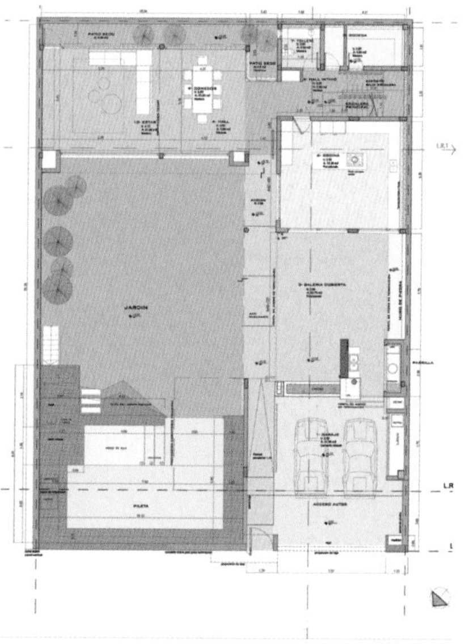
JARDIN
PILETA
LR
L

Minimalist elegance,
clad in Italian stone in
calming shades of gray.

The **pools collect** rainwater, which **cascades** to **create** a **natural cooling** system in a **hot** climate.

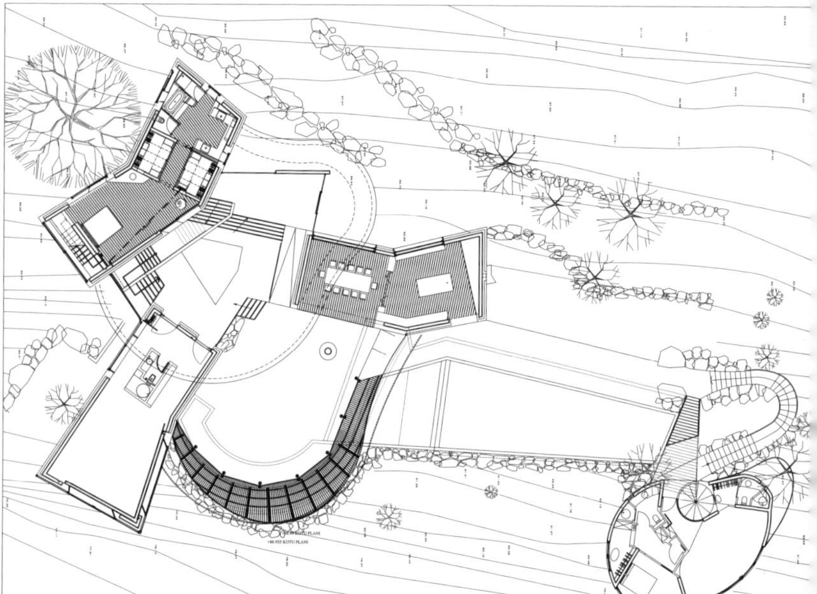

+88.935 KOTU PLANI

Two roof-top terrace pools, with spectacular views of the city and the surrounding mountains.

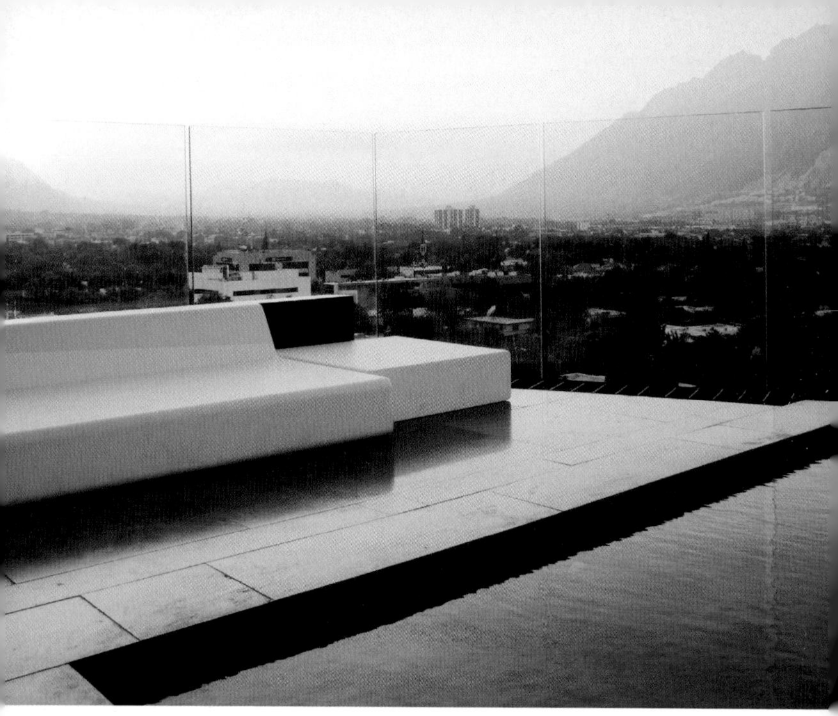

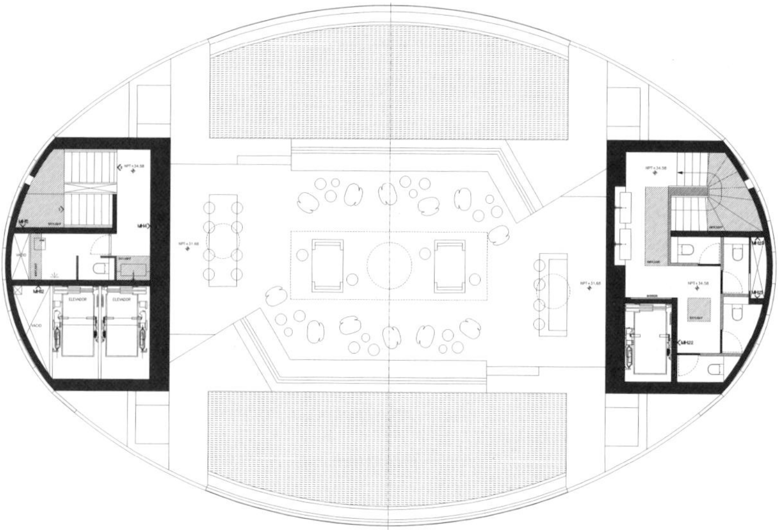

NPT + 34.58
VACIO
ELEVADOR
ELEVADOR
NPT + 31.68
NPT + 34.58
NPT + 31.68
NPT + 34.58

A bathing and wellness landscape that respects the historical aspect.

Spectacular views of Lake Constance
from the interior pools allow a
unique bathing experience.

sinne

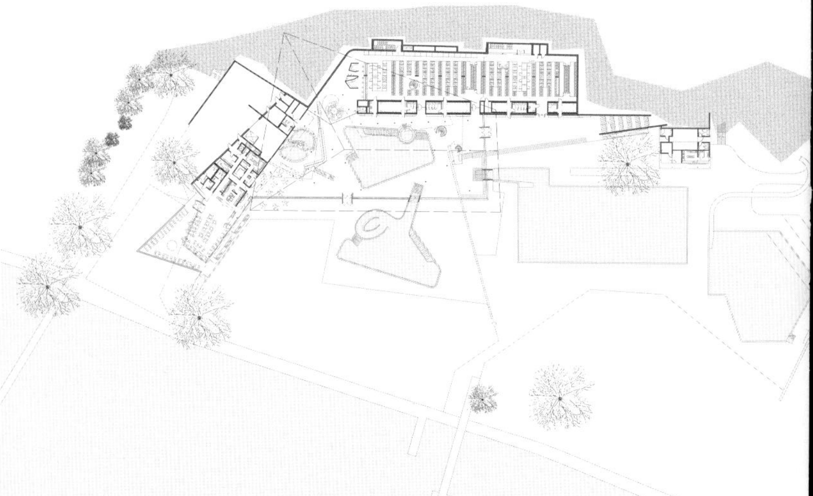

wärme

sauna

The **architectural** lake element re-stages the **varieties** of the existing **water world** and adds new ones.

2
1
3
7
8
4
10
1
9
12
5
6
13
11
1

Lap and recreation pools connect the ocean with the house, bridging the gap between water and desert.

All areas of the pool are interpreted
as zones of a single body
coated homogenously
with polyester.

The superimposed **volumes** are **aligned** with the **pool.**

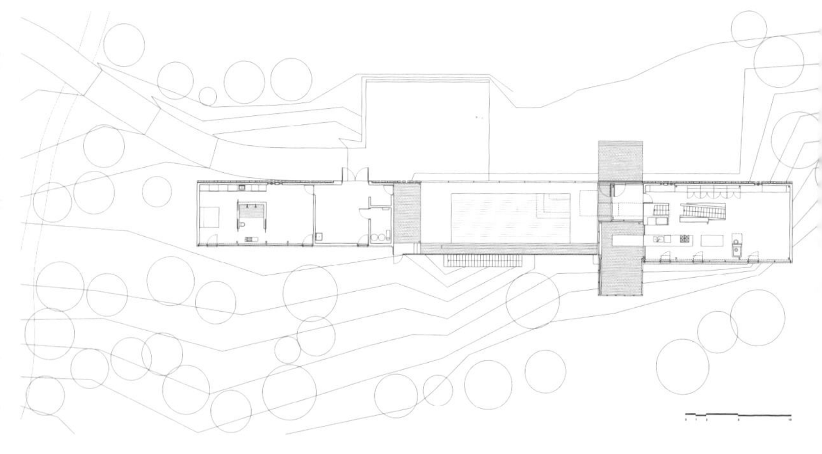

Extending beyond the building
lines over the streets
of Dallas.
3FT-6IN

3 FT-6IN
NO DIVING
3 FT-6IN
3 FT-6IN

4 FT-6 IN
4 FT-6 IN

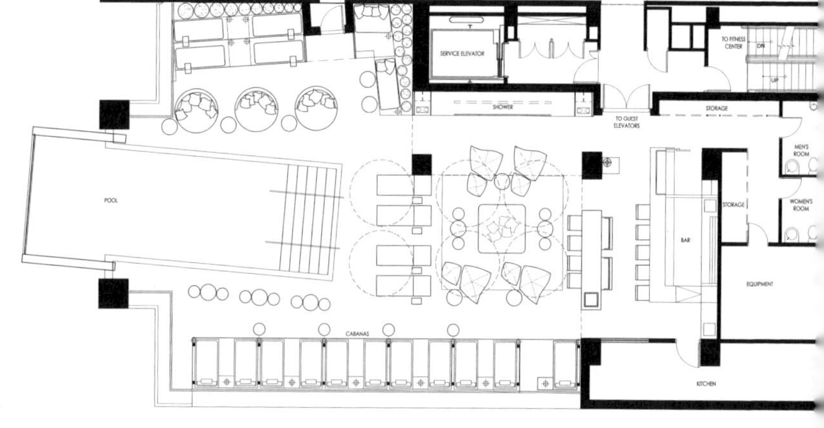

SERVICE ELEVATOR
SHOWER
TO FITNESS CENTER
DN
UP
TO GUEST ELEVATORS
STORAGE
MEN'S ROOM
WOMEN'S ROOM
POOL
STORAGE
BAR
EQUIPMENT
CABANAS
KITCHEN

3 FT-6IN
3 FT-6IN

The lagoon holds the
Guinness World Record
for the largest swimming
pool in the world.

A thermal therapy experience
that engages each
of the body's senses.

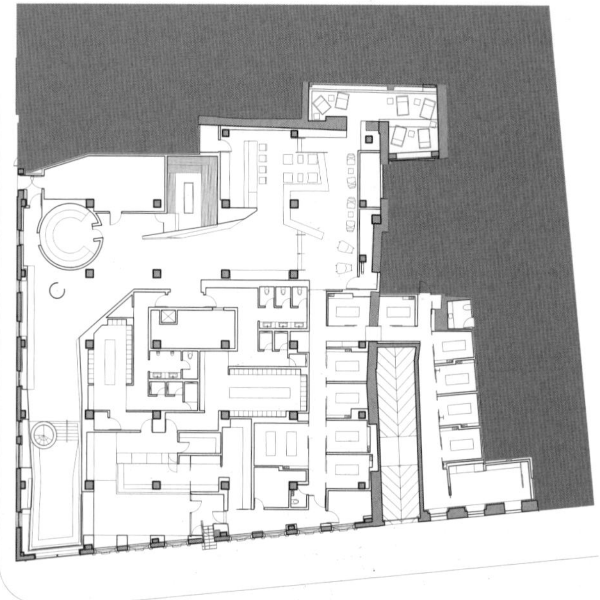

Five colors correspond to the five senses stimulated by this spa experience.

RUHEpol

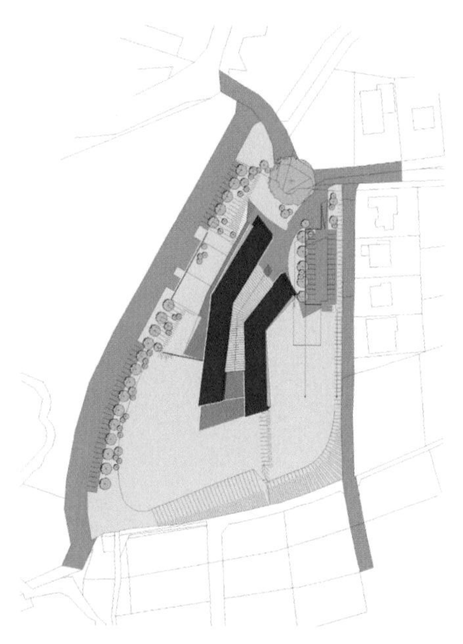

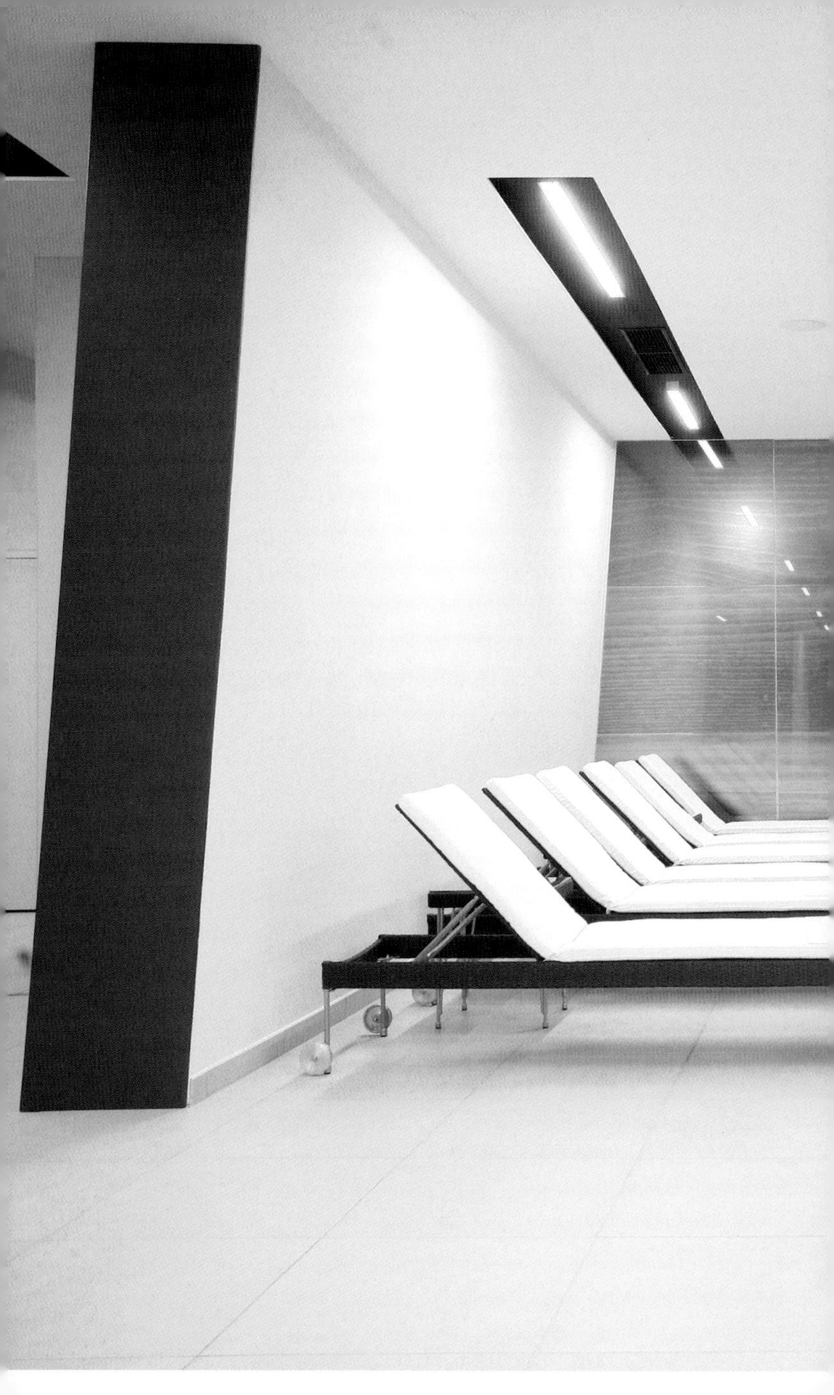

With its **green** façades and **roof**, Sportplaza Mercator seems like an **overgrown fortress.**

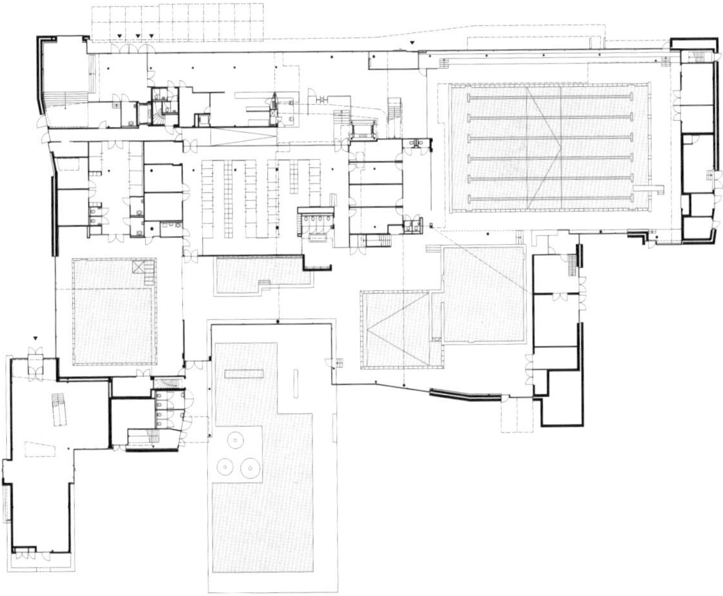

PEPSI

The **building** volume has a monumental **character**, **emerging** as a man-made **forest** from the landscape.

A mobile recreation pier for underserved waterfront communities.

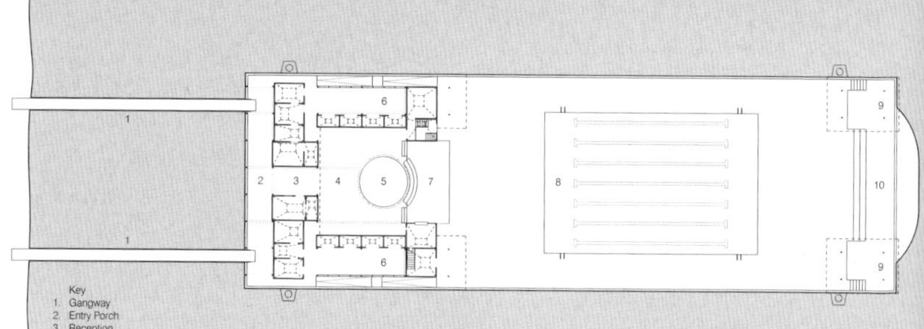
1
1
2
3
4
5
6
6
7
8
9
9
10
Key
1. Gangway
2. Entry Porch
3. Reception
4. Deck
5. Waterplay
6. Changing Area
7. Dining Terrace
8. Pool
9. Shade Pavilion
10. Stage

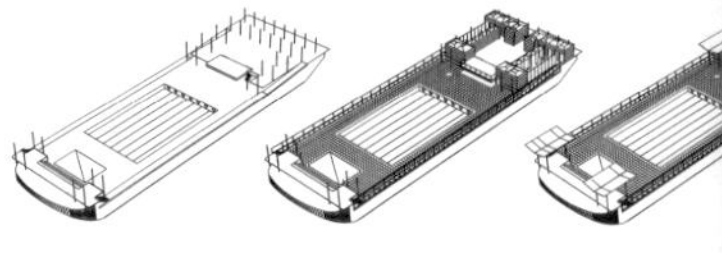

PLAN

MANAGER

Spectacular
360° panoramic views.

Contrasting the traditional
with the contemporary.

Each **dome** has a distinctly individual character.

10
20

A **visual** and **physical continuum** between **indoors** and **outdoors.**

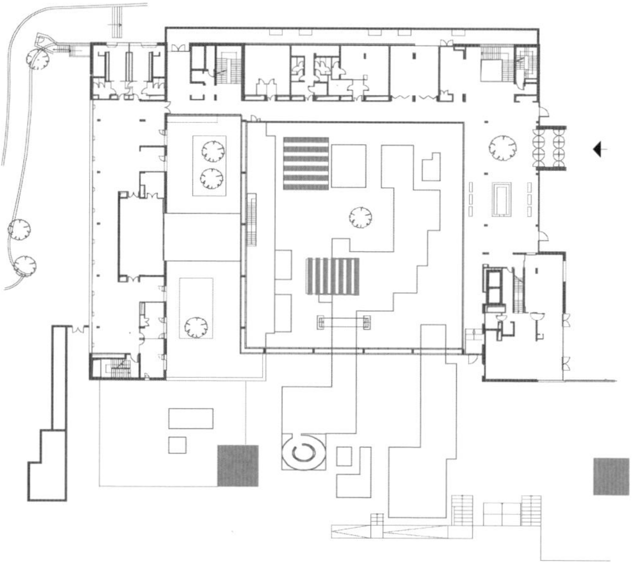

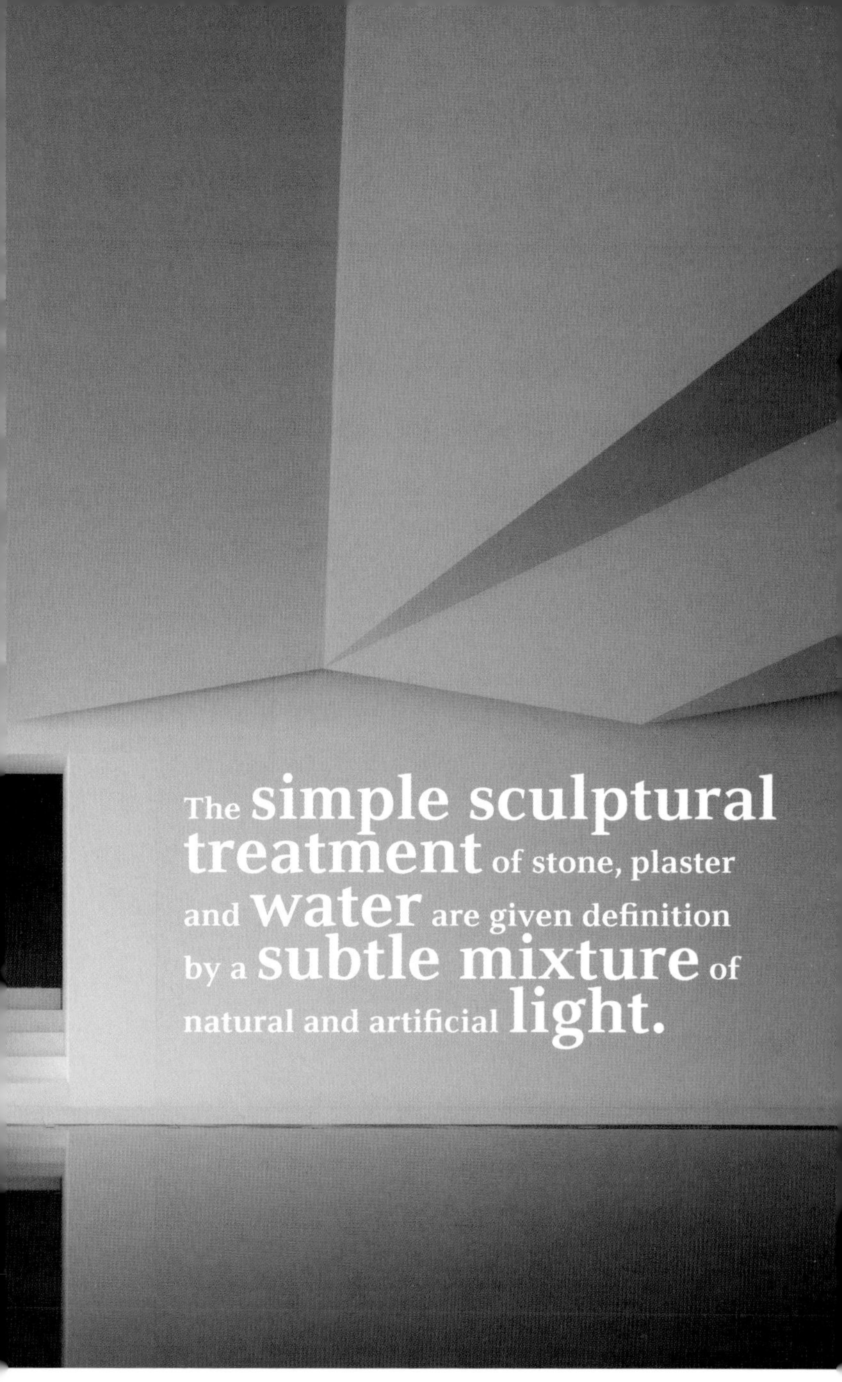

The **simple sculptural treatment** of stone, plaster and **water** are given definition by a **subtle mixture** of natural and artificial **light.**

Designed as part of the
underground spa,
this pool is far more than
a body of water.

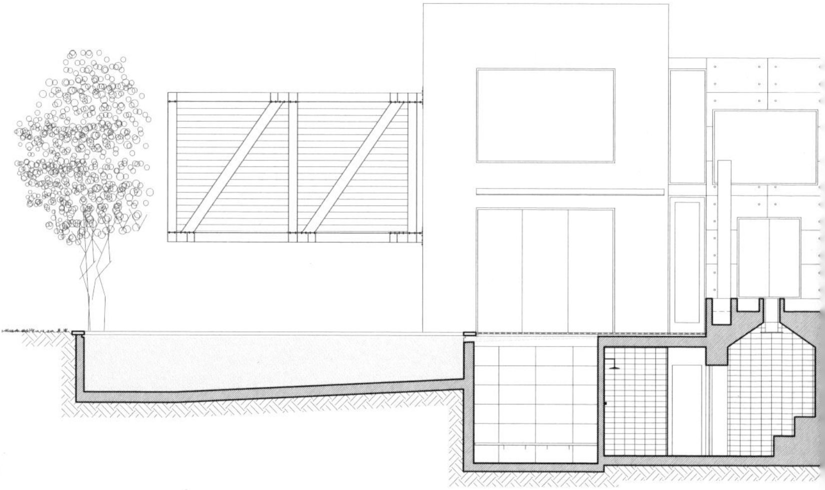

The resort interacts in a unique way with surrounding nature.

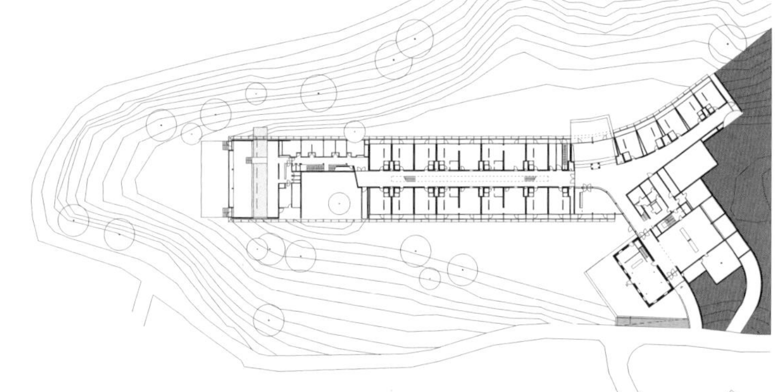

Transparent, smooth transitions
coupled with warm materials,
powerful shades of color and
special light effects.

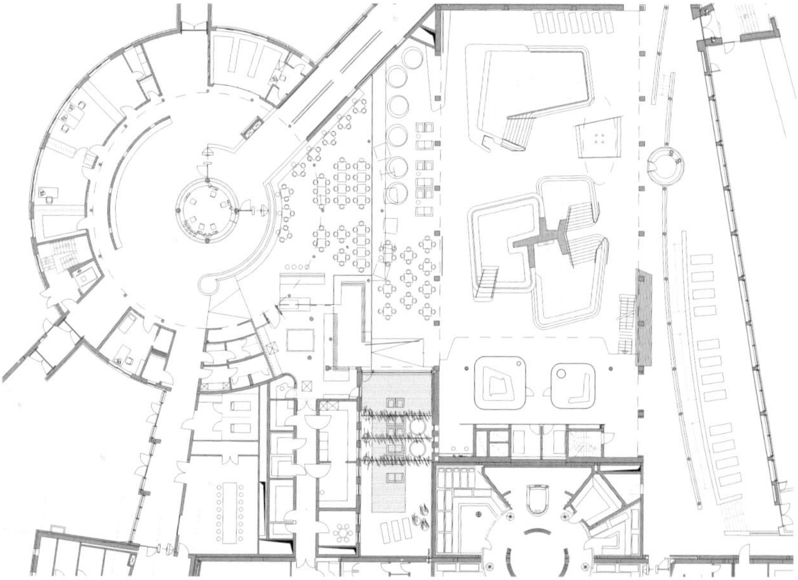

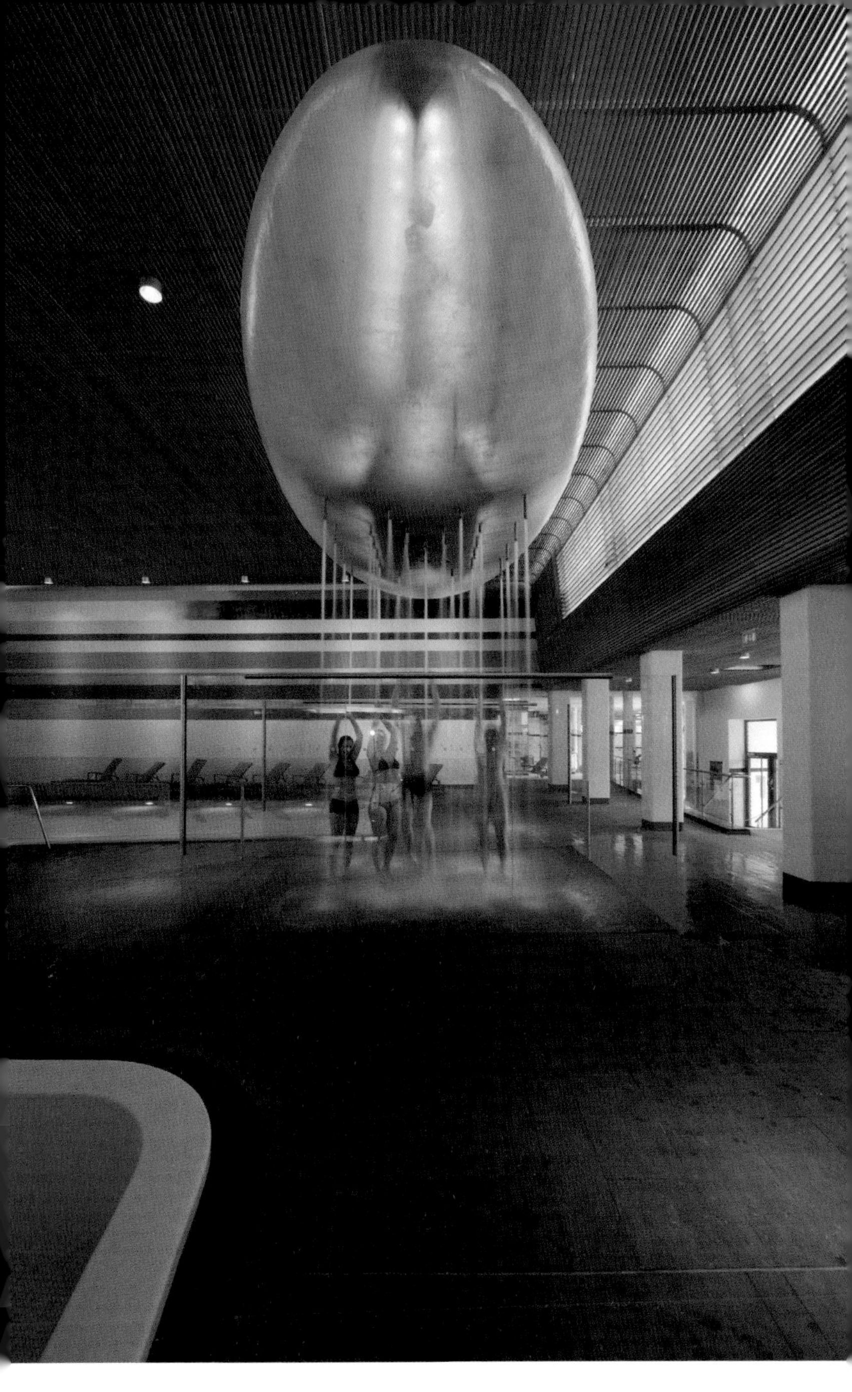

The concept combines the symbolism of the square in Chinese culture and the natural structure of soap bubbles.

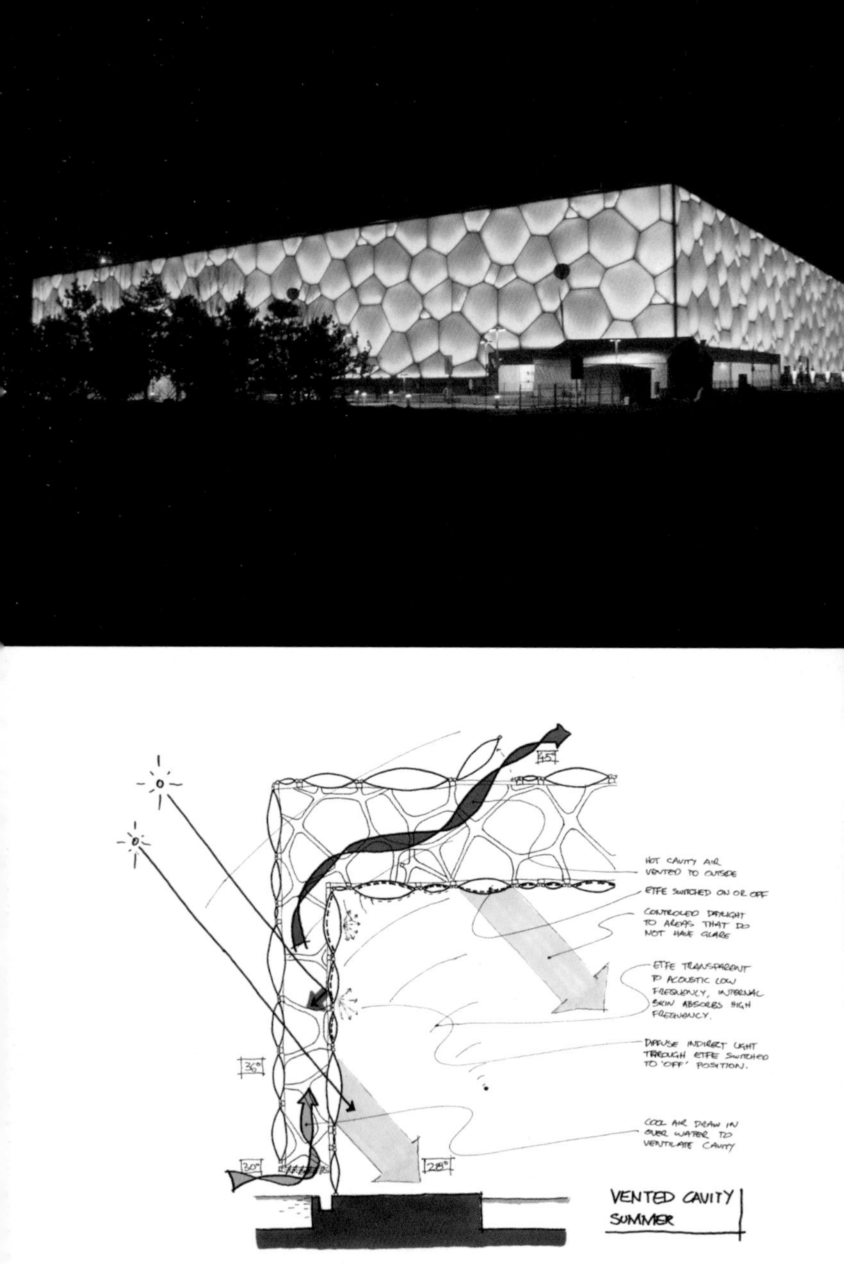
45°
HOT CAVITY AIR VENTED TO OUTSIDE
ETFE SWITCHED ON OR OFF
CONTROLED DAYLIGHT TO AREAS THAT DO NOT HAVE GLARE
ETFE TRANSPARENT TO ACOUSTIC LOW FREQUENCY, INTERNAL SKIN ABSORBS HIGH FREQUENCY.
DIFFUSE INDIRECT LIGHT THROUGH ETFE SWITCHED TO 'OFF' POSITION.
36°
COOL AIR DRAW IN OVER WATER TO VENTILATE CAVITY
30°
28°
VENTED CAVITY
SUMMER

WOMEN'S 100M BACK WR
HEAT 3
1 (4) SZEPESI N. HUN 1:08
2 (5) LIAO YALI CHN 1:07
3 (2) BATJARGAL MGL 1:08
4 (3) PRILEPA A. KAZ 1:08
5 (8) CHUI L. MAS 1:08
6 (7) TAN CHI YAN MAC 1:10
Nikon

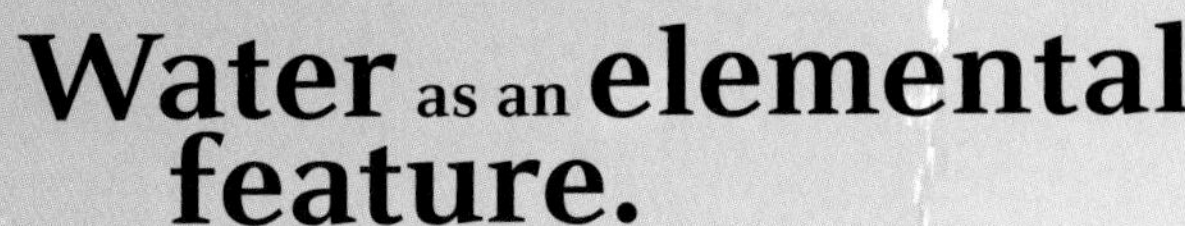

Water as an elemental feature.

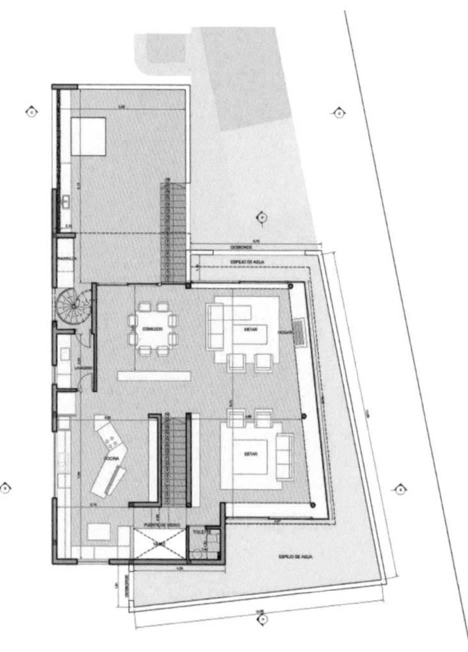

DESBORDE
ESPEJO DE AGUA
PARRILLA
COMEDOR
ESTAR
HOGAR
LAVADERO
COCINA
ESTAR
PUENTE DE VIDRIO
TOILETTE
ESPEJO DE AGUA

The concept is that of
a sanctuary – a place
to escape.

40 m

1.40 m

The outside pool interacts
with the living room, both
becoming one whole
dynamic space.

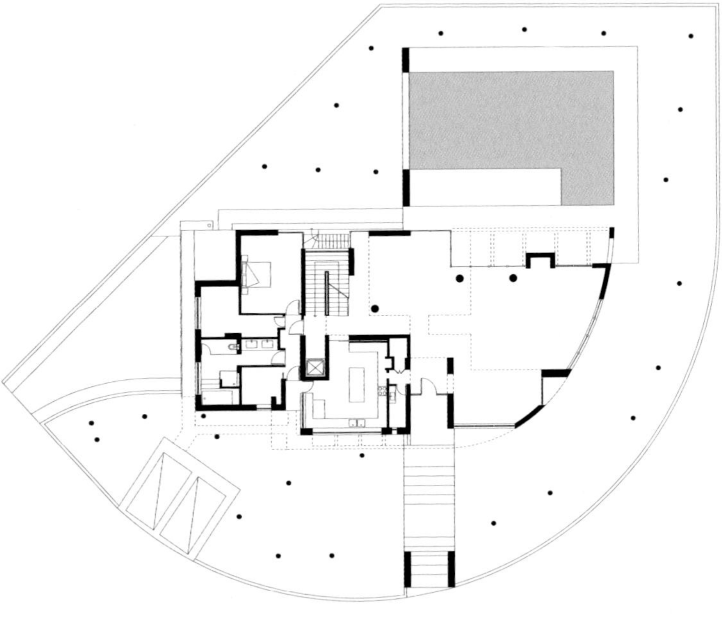

The pool house hovers
over the pool like
a vessel in the water.

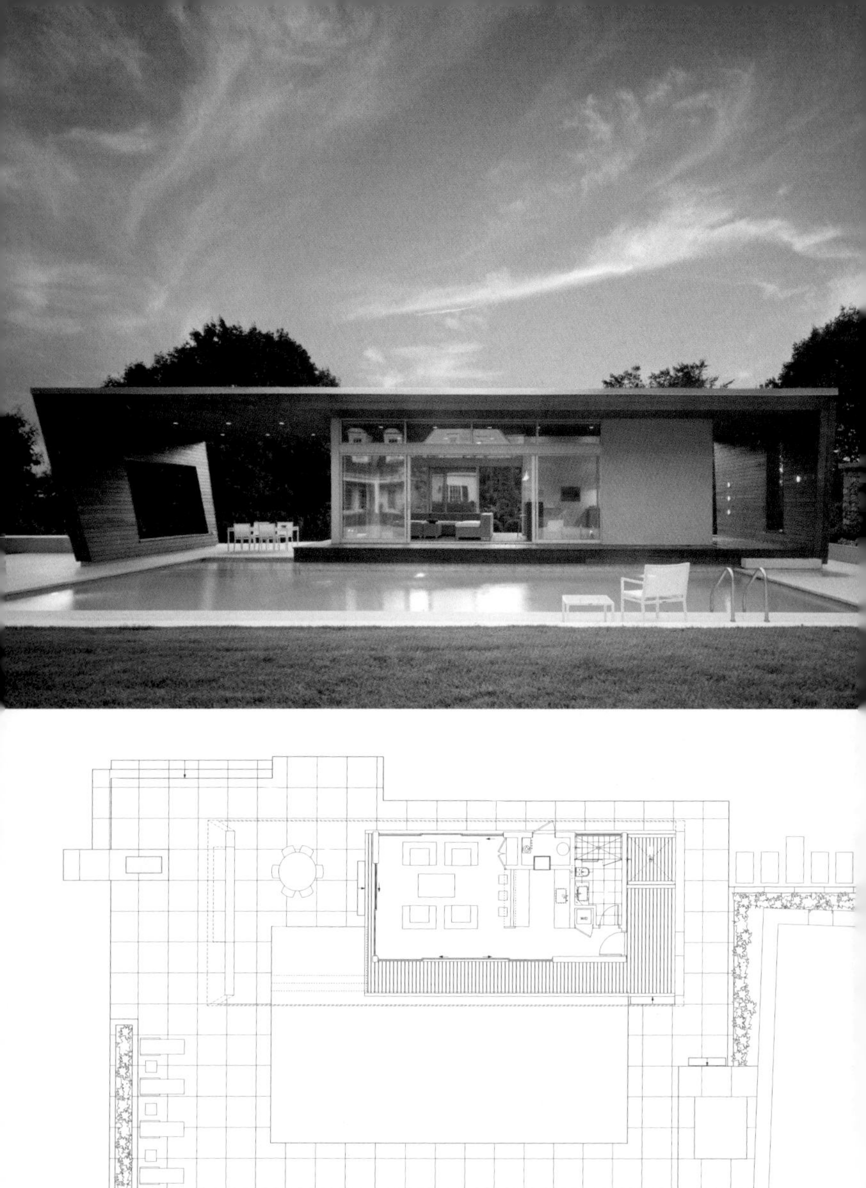

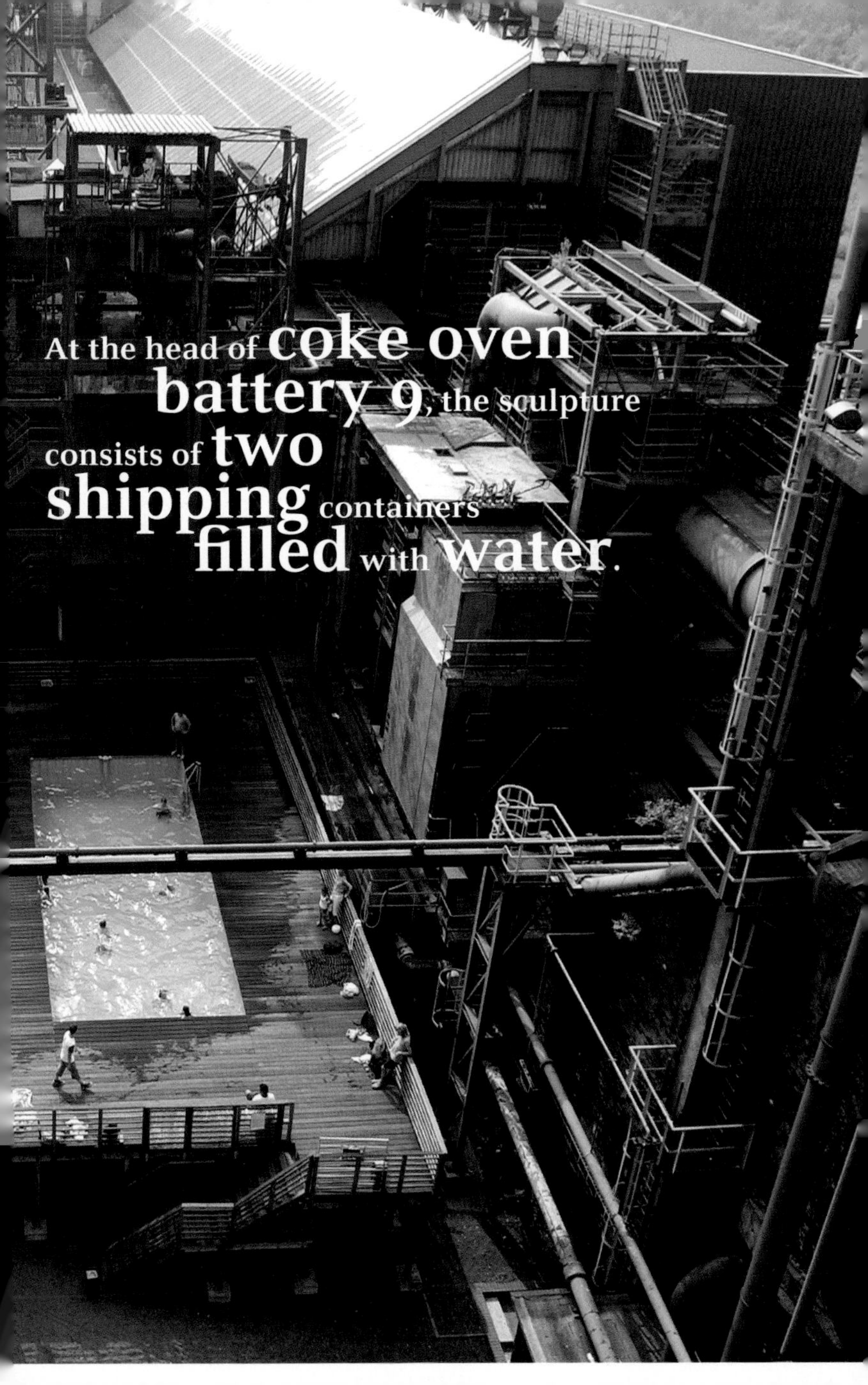
At the head of coke oven battery 9, the sculpture consists of two shipping containers filled with water.

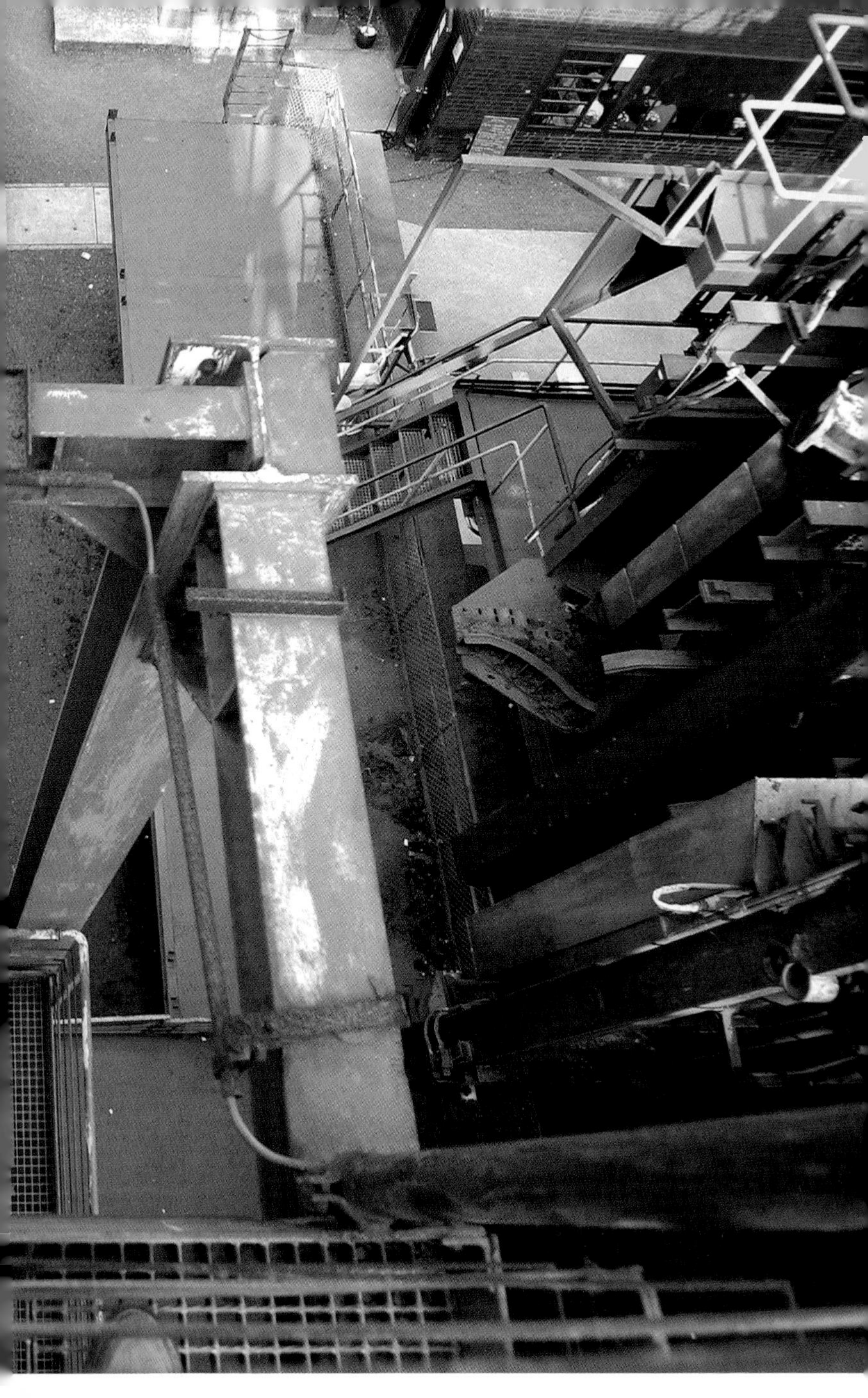

Architects Index

Picture Credits

Alila Cha Am 28-33
archisphere/ Balance Resort Stegersbach 78-83
Baumann, Philippe 276-283
Behnisch Architekten, Photos Adam Mørk, Torben Eskerod 298-309
Bekman, Ali 152-157
Bernath, Roland 266-275
BIG 120-121, 123, 131
Bitter Bredt Fotografie 92-99
Bitter, Jan 170-171, 173 a.
Bulot, Marc-Antoine 146-151
Cano, ENRICO 364-369
CHOIon Photography 204-211
Chrystal Lagoons 238-241
Cramer, Marc 222-229, 242-249
Dalhoff, Casper 122
Design Hotels™ 34-42, 84-91, 132-137, 284-289
Adrien Dirand, courtesy of HABITA Monterrey 166-169
Ditz, Uwe 184-185, 192-193, 340-347
Eheim, Jürgen 58-67
Goula, Adrià 106-113
Guillaume, Clement 48-57
Hawkes, Jason 290-291
He, Shu 158-159, 160 b., 161-163
House Owner/ Pollensa 68-73
Kasper, Guido 186-191
Klab Architecture 372-381
Kramer, Luuk 258-265
Dr Krieger Architekten + Ingenieure 176-183
Laignel, Eric 230-237
Mettelsiefen, Marcell 74-77
Morgado, Joao 172, 173 b., 174-175
Musi, Pino 370-371
Orkelbog-Andrsen, Leif 128-129
Ott, Paul 212-221
Peral, Alejandro 100-105, 138-145, 356-357, 360, 362-363
Undine Pröhl, courtesy of HABITA Monterrey 164-165
PTW Architects, John Pauline
PTW Architects 348-355
Ramirez, Elsa 326-131
Rana, Juan 358-359, 361
Lukas Schaller 194-203
De Smedt, Julien 124-127
Stein, Isa 250-257
Stiftung Industriedenkmalpflege/ Manfred Vollmer, Zollverein coking plant Essen 390-397
Summer, Edmund 292-297
Swalwell, Derek 12-19
Vigilius Mountain Resort, Georg Tappeiner, Design Hotels 332-339
Warchol, Paul 114-117, 119, 382-389
White, Hillary Ferris 118
Xerra, Gionata 310-317
Xiangyu, Sun 160 a.
Zaini, Fabrice - Serero architects42-47

Cover:
Alila Cha Am